SOUTHAMPTON
PAST & PRESENT

JOHN EDGAR MANN

NEW PHOTOGRAPHS BY
PATRICK BROOKES
AND
PHILIP BURNER

COUNTRYSIDE BOOKS
NEWBURY

First Published 1985
©John Edgar Mann

COUNTRYSIDE BOOKS
3 CATHERINE ROAD
NEWBURY, BERKSHIRE

ISBN 0 905392 53 1

Dedication
To Tony Brode

Designed and typeset by Publicity Plus, Newbury
Printed and bound in Great Britain by Woodnough Bookbinding
Limited, Wellingborough
Produced through MRM (Print Consultants) Reading

INTRODUCTION

Southampton has a low profile, rather like its natives. I have heard 'immigrants' dub Sotonians 'doorsteppers' - meaning that you don't get beyond your neighbour's doorstep very often. But this is surely just old fashioned caution on the part of the 'Moosh'. Southampton is actually a very warm community and its people are generally fiercely proud of their city. This book shows the changes which have come about over the last hundred years. The buildings may have changed but the people who live here have not. Once a 'Moosh' takes you to his heart he's a friend for life.

If in the past neither the city nor its people have engendered deserved enthusiasm, it could be because Southampton has long been thought of as a place one passes through on the way to France, America and more exotic locations. 'Gateway to the Empire' a northern boundary sign once proclaimed. The disadvantage of a gateway is that people go through it and don't stop. But if you were to stop, having failed somehow to miss that information bureau which tends to interrupt the Bargate vista, you may still have a difficult job finding the city's most interesting places. For Southampton isn't compact: it sprawls, and offers excellent exercise! But the search is rewarding. Southampton waits for people to creep up on it, and for those who take the trouble to look, the city has much of interest to offer.

Southampton, despite its contemporary look, is very old indeed. Its 2,000 year old history as a port has been full of drama. Like that Sunday morning in 1338 when the French raided the town while its citizens were at worship.

If the walls of its oldest church, St Michael's, could speak they would tell of parishioners slaughtered as they left the mass. After the sacking of Southampton the town remained ruined for many years.

The Black Death of a decade later hardly helped its fortunes, but at least the French raids led to the building of the fortifications we can still see today. Historians have called them the most impressive example of medieval urban defence in England, and refer to the Bargate as Britain's finest town gateway. The walls remain remarkable both to look at and to walk upon.

Greater prosperity came at the beginning of the sixteenth century with the rise in overseas trade in wool, though fortunes fell again not so much due to the collapse of trade with the Mediterranean as to the growth of London as a commercial centre. The seventeenth century merely consolidated the gloom. The Civil War denuded the town of its money and the Great Plague of its people.

It wasn't the sea trade which brought prosperity back to the port but that eighteenth century enthusiasm for spa waters. Southampton had the twin advantages of beneficial springs and the other health fad of those times - sea water. It was fortuitous that the town should have become fashionable, if only briefly, at a time of economic decline. Aristocrats and even some Royals rented houses here and later wealthy merchants built stately homes nearby.

The town grew apace. The next century was to bring about a revolution in steam traffic: docks and railways interlocked in mutual benefit. Soon Southampton became famous the world over as a passenger port. The 'unsinkable' *Titanic,* symbol of the confident heyday of the liners, went down on its maiden voyage in 1912, widowing and orphaning many a Southampton home. Greater leviathans were to follow, but things were never quite the same after that disaster.

Around the turn of the century and in the years that followed adjoining villages were turning into suburbs, and what was already happening in London began to happen here. Country lanes gradually filled up with houses and shops, and estates appeared where once the gentry strolled, oblivious to encroaching social revolution. But the new suburbs with village centres retained much of their old character. Even today, despite physical changes, some cling tenaciously to their village roots.

N.V.B.

ACKNOWLEDGEMENTS

During the period in which I have been engaged on these excursions into the past of my native city I have had great assistance from many new, as well as old, friends. My heartfelt thanks go to local historian A.G.K. Leonard in particular who was kind enough to cast a critical eye over the manuscript and make many constructive suggestions. Jack Foley, the acknowledged local expert on the postcards of the splendidly named Francis Godolphin Osborne Stuart, helped me in dating not only the Stuarts but also in approximating the dates of other cards and photographs too. In the initial stages both Bill White and Jeff Pain were especially helpful.

I have tried to choose unfamiliar cards and photos and to avoid those previously published in local history books and booklets. Dating where possible is precise, but some experts may cavil at the use of the ubiquitous c. for circa (g. for guess!). Some of the later photographs lacked credits and their sources were difficult to trace, so my apologies if I have trodden on any professional toes.

The following were kind enough to let me borrow cards, photos and prints: Bill White, Jeff Pain, Ian Abrahams and the Bitterne Local History Society, Terry Gregory, John Stockley, Brian Ticehurst, George Gregory, Roy Martin, Bruce and Angela Gilbert, Rosemary Horobin, George Timms, Jim Love, Cyril Saunders, my stepmother Ruth Mann and my employers Southern Newspapers PLC.

I hope readers will get as much pleasure and enjoyment from looking at these remarkable views of our city as I have had in compiling them.

JOHN EDGAR MANN

CONTENTS

MESSENGER BOYS, dangerously close to a wet drop, look camerawards on Ocean Dock (opened in 1911). In the background: the liner *Olympic,* sister ship of the ill-fated *Titanic.* This postcard was inaccurately captioned 'Trafalgar Dock'.

THE DOCKS 1985

THE OCEAN TERMINAL later occupied the site of the White Star sheds (seen opposite). Now the terminal, too, has gone, and with it the era of the big liners. The photo shows the brigantine *Soren Larsen,* converted for a disabled crew, and Tribal class frigates being refitted for the Indonesian Navy.

TIMES WERE HARD for some, but when this photo was taken of the dock gate beside the imposing post office there was much activity - and only one person, the lad crossing the road on the right, seems to have spotted the cameraman.

WHERE HAS ALL the traffic gone? One could almost add —Long time passing! The port has seen its passenger heyday, and the time of the containers is here. Now the docks post office has a new British Telecom role.

AN UNUSUAL PHOTO displaying facade-ruining signs, including one for the station's less familiar name. Fortunately the facia boards were taken down later—the London and South Western Railway became part of the Southern Railway in the 1923 re-grouping.

SIR WILLIAM TITE'S famous building, which drew praise from Sir John Betjeman, was closed in 1966 but briefly reopened for pre-Christmas rush goods traffic. It has been in a sorry semi-derelict state for years, but at the time of writing there are plans to turn it into a casino and restaurant.

OPENED AS the Imperial in 1867, this magnificent hotel was soon taken over by the LSWR and had a name change. As the South Western it became one of the world's most famous hotels, comparable with Shepheard's in Cairo. This unusual photo reveals that on the corner facing towards the Royal Pier you could once see right through to the Terminus Station.

SOUTH WESTERN HOTEL 1985

THE STATELY caravanserai where once tycoons, film stars and crowned heads luxuriated before and after the London boat train now houses offices and most notably a BBC studio. It ceased to be a hotel when the last war broke out, and became a naval shore base, HMS Shrapnel. As to peeping through to the Terminus, that ended soon after our earlier picture was taken.

IN 1887 the Missions to Seamen, whose Southampton HQ had been in an adapted house at Town Quay, merged with the local Waterside Mission, taking over their Royal Crescent premises. Here they remained until the 1930s when the opening of the Western Docks prompted the purchase of a Queen's Terrace site closer to the heart of things.

THE IVY-CLAD Seamen's Mission may not have been a wonder of architecture, but it would have looked very impressive beside this aircraft hangar. And that is really what the building is—the city's Hall of Aviation (formerly the Mitchell Museum) with an entrance in Albert Road. The sea has given way to air.

THE ESPLANADE c. 1904

A CONTEMPORARY hotel brochure, listing 'the largest pier in the South of England' as one of Southampton's top attractions, pointed out that there was accommodation for ten steamers and that 'the beautiful pavilion at the pierhead' seated a thousand people. So no wonder there was work for this line of horse cabs. The scene has a curiously Continental air, but then the card was published by a wide-ranging French company.

THE PIER area is still pleasant and the 'new' Mayflower Park attracts large numbers of ozone inhalers and sun worshippers if the day is a good one. But the noise of motors has replaced that of horseshoes and the once fashionable pier is closed—doubtless forever. A little of the old atmosphere came back during the Tall Ships Week when the port briefly became what it has always half-heartedly aspired to be—a resort.

PADDLE STEAMERS abounded and there was even a pier railway, though passenger traffic ended with the First World War. The pier was opened on July 8th 1833, when the teenaged Princess Victoria and her mother the Duchess of Kent came down to open 'a noble edifice 900 feet long with a drive 20 feet wide for 50 carriages'.

IT WAS REBUILT twice within 60 years — c.1840 (wooden piles had been eaten away by the shrimp-like gribbles) and in the early 1890s when there was a cast-iron replacement. Though the pier is shut, forlorn, decayed and almost certainly doomed, the gatehouse of 1926, replacing the one of 1892, has been saved, with plans to turn it into a restaurant and pub.

THE POSTCARD dubs it The Old Quay Castle (called South Castle in Corporation papers). The old jail was then covered by creeper, serving as a backcloth to an ill-fated terracotta statue of Prince Albert which was removed in 1907 . . . lest the visiting Kaiser be upset by the shabby condition of a memorial to his grandfather! It was stored in the Corporation's West Quay yard and broken up in 1914 by soldiers in a display of anti-German zeal.

IN 1960 the Corporation restored the ancient building, which was the headquarters of the town gunner at the time of Henry V. In 1775 it was converted into a jail but had ceased to function in this capacity in 1855 when a new town jail was built in Ascupart Street. Now the tower serves as an archaeological museum.

IT DOESN'T seem all that long ago that trains were puffing up and down at the bottom of High Street.

THE TRAINS have gone but not the rails. The tall building, Geddes' Warehouse (a grain store in the old days), is now a luxury flats development.

WEST QUAY c.1930

A VIEW of Western Parade from the water. To the left of here were the fashionable bathing venues of Southampton's brief period as a spa. There are three memorials in a row—the water trough recording the family of distinguished local lady Madame Maes, whose home was at this spot; then the 1901 'Stella' memorial to the brave stewardess of a wrecked ship; and finally 1913's tall tribute to the Pilgrim Fathers who sailed from the port.

24

THE MEMORIALS remain and so does the Royal Southern Yacht Club building (extreme right), now the headquarters of Southampton University Air Squadron. It has always provided a splendid vantage point for photographers and is certainly the waterfront's most attractive building — a splendid example of the Italian style favoured by Victorian architects.

THE WESTERN SHORE 1906

THESE TWO PICTURES demonstrate the changes wrought by 80 years. When F.G.O. Stuart took this shot, Western Shore meant just that and the view from the Royal Southern Yacht Club was truly impressive. You could look right across the water to the West, now Central, Station.

A PRESENT-DAY POSTCARD could not carry the same title. The shore line has moved away to the south and where once was an expanse of water are now docks, factories, a modern hotel . . . and people sun themselves in what were the gardens behind the walls.

H.E. LOCKE'S painting makes up in charm what it lacks in fidelity—one church spire looks too big and the other far too small. But the painter did convey a nice idea of how charming a stroll along the esplanade would have been.

A FIVE-TIER CAR PARK, multi-storey blocks and Pirelli-General's factory have savaged a once delightful spot. Only Forest View, that still attractive 1868 terrace perched on the old walls, remains an observable survivor from Locke's painting.

THE IMPOSING structure with Barling's beer wagon inappropriately parked outside it was the forerunner of Southampton University—the Hartley Institution, upgraded prematurely to university in the postcard caption (it was then a university college). Of the buildings shown on the left nothing remains: on the right, survivors include the city's oldest pub building, the Red Lion, and the GPO.

POUPARTS, the fruit and veg importers, have replaced the old Hartley, but passers-by are reminded of the site's academic past by a wall plaque recalling that the Institution stood there from 1862 to 1936, becoming a university college in 1902. It was founded under the will of Henry Robinson Hartley, whose house stood on the spot until 1862.

'WHERE THE policeman is standing is one of Bert's point duties,' wrote the correspondent of this postcard, noting that Bert's colleague had a white cover on his hat because it was summer. His point was Holy Rood, opposite the embassy-like 1867 National Westminster Bank (as it now is). The spire is that of St. Lawrence's Church, demolished a year later for a now more common reason—redundancy.

GONE ARE the clanging trams—and most of the activity. If 'Main Street' is split in two by the medieval gateway, then the lower part is now the poor, if senior, relation. Little remains of the old High Street on the left, though the bank looks as impressive as ever—the most elegant building in the city? The right side of the street has fared better.

HIGH STREET 1812

THIS WATER COLOUR *Taken from Bar Gate,* shows why the thoroughfare drew so much praise from visiting writers. Time and adversity have wrought many changes, few aesthetically pleasing. Notice the tower above the last building on the right - a reminder of the Marquis of Lansdowne's short-lived sham-Gothic castle (1804-1818).

THE EARLY nineteenth century artist let his detail tail away as the fine vista receded south, but the spire of Southampton's oldest building, St. Michael's, is visible in both old and new views - and that's about all that is! The bow windows of the old coaching inn, the Dolphin, can just be glimpsed jutting out (centre, left).

A QUAINT corner in more delightful days—more delightful pictorially, of course. Here in Westgate Street beavered the circular saw inventor Walter Taylor (1734-1803) and in the spa period the gateway led to popular bathing establishments. At one time the gatehouse was a residence.

THE WEST GATE 1985

HOW THE Post House Hotel ruins the view! The Westgate Street architecture of recent years suits the old town less effectively than the new housing in nearby Bugle Street. Indeed, the main merit in the present-day scene is the view it provides of the restored Tudor Merchants' Hall where, among other events, poetry readings are held.

THE OXFORD Street corner hums with activity—and not only with activity, to judge by the street sweeper brushing up the omnipresent horse manure and the lad advancing with his pan from the dung-cart. There were plenty of shops in Bernard Street in those days, and yet it wasn't really a top shopping thoroughfare. Is that a ticket collector on the open deck of the tram?

BERNARD STREET 1985

THE FORMER Bridge Street has come a long way since it was named after the bridge that once spanned the town ditch. What is now, and since 1924, Bernard Street in its entirety at one time consisted of three highways: Bridge Street, Bernard Street and Itchen Bridge Road. By far the most interesting part today is its eastern end (out of shot in our photos) where early Victorian houses have undergone renovation.

THE LAND'S finest medieval town gateway might have wound up as an American tourist attraction like the Queen Mary or London Bridge. But that turn-of-the-century solution to traffic problems was fortunately abandoned and specially built tramcars rattled through the arch instead. This photograph shows the first completed side of an oft-mooted circus.

THE BARGATE 1985

THE WESTERN side of the circus was completed in 1938 and the last tram passed under the arch on June 4th of that year. Now the old gate looks out on a precinct instead of a thoroughfare and the trams that went through a decade before made their last journeys in 1949.

PROBABLY TAKEN in the late 1920s or early 1930s, this interesting high-angle photo of unknown date shows more vehicles than people. In a few years time the west side, depicted here, would be a bomb site.

NOW IT'S a case of more people and no vehicles. The post-war architecture was planned so as not to dwarf the Bargate (which, even if flanked by skyscrapers would still be a stand-out). What is missing today is the pleasing higgledy piggledy character of Above Bar's pre-war frontages.

BEHIND THE Clock Tower, bequeathed in 1889 by a lady whose concern for animals was reflected in its troughs for horses, cattle and dogs, was Moira House, then occupied by a draper, and behind that the equally elegant Georgian facade of Moira Place, which had a brief notoriety in 1856 when the footman at No. 1 murdered the 'upper' housemaid in a crime passionnel. The scandal drew discreet headlines and lengthy reports in the national press.

TWENTY-ONE years ago Moira House came down, to be replaced by a modern building housing the Nationwide Building Society. A Ministry inspector decided that the old house was of insufficient architectural quality to be preserved. Many townsfolk disagreed. The Clock Tower, considered a traffic hazard, disappeared even earlier, in 1934, to reappear at Bitterne Park Triangle where it overlooks the Itchen.

PROUD SOUTHAMPTON'S famed hymnologist (1674-1748), whose lines 'How doth the little busy bee improve each shining hour,' etc. were taught—are they still?—to generations of improvable children, stands within long-vanished railings with his back to a Cumberland Place which has a more charming facade than today's.

NOW ISAAC stands in front of a modern office block and his greatest hit, 'Our God Our Help in Ages Past,' chimes out regularly from the nearby Civic Centre clock. The Victorian statue, if not the greatest hit of eccentric local sculptor R.C. Lucas (1800-1883), who drove a chariot round the town clad in a toga, is arguably that artist's best-known work.

LONDON ROAD (SOUTH) c. 1935

A VIVID picture of everyday life in the upper reaches of the town's business centre, an area, then as now, to go to for house sales or purchases. Projecting over the pavement on the left (opposite the tram) is the canopy of the long-gone Carlton Cinema, opened in 1915.

THE HOUSES on the left have lost their railings and a post-war facade leads up to the Carlton Crescent turning. Changes, too, on the right, a notable omission being the blitzed St. Paul's Church, built in 1829. But somehow despite the differences, London Road retains its distinctive 'office' character.

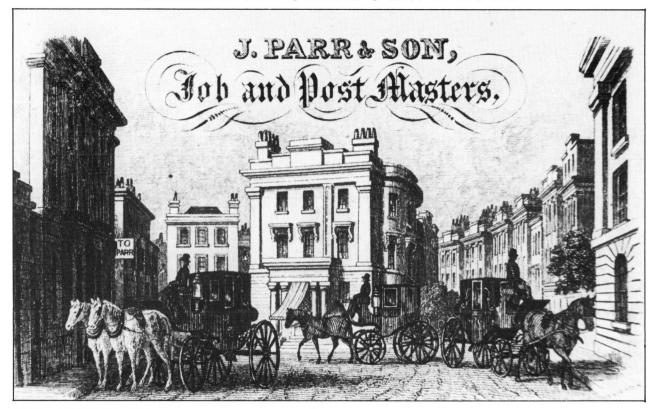

THIS ADVERTISEMENT comes from the 1853 Post Office Directory and refers to just one of half a dozen town centre posting masters in the half-century before the horseless carriage. The engraving is by the indefatigable Philip Brannon. Winchester Street is to the left (note sign: 'To Parr').

CARLTON CRESCENT 1985

MUCH REMAINS. The building on the corner of Carlton Place and what was then called The Crescent (an echo of Bath!) is by ironical contrast devoted to car hire, has gained a frontal extension and lost its fancy top. Buildings to the left are extant — it's a pity about that modern building in Carlton Place!

THIS F.G.O. STUART CARD is captioned 'Ordnance Survey Office, Southampton' — its buildings lie beyond the National Provincial Bank of England at the corner of Carlton Crescent. Opposite, on the corner of Bellevue Road, is another bank — Lloyds.

GONE ARE HORSE CABS and the tram. The elegant NP branch is now Nat West, but north of it most of the OSO buildings have vanished — the Survey HQ is at Maybush now. The Lloyds site is a new building (though named Old Bank House) and Lloyds branch is at present to the south on the left, out of shot.

THE CIVIC CENTRE was still being built, with work on the tower incomplete. The municipal offices opened in 1932 and the law courts the following year. The Guildhall, library and art gallery were yet to come. Many landmarks have since gone: The Grand Theatre, the Coliseum, the old King Edward School.

'WHAT HITLER BEGAN, planners completed'. Looking at our two pictures, taken from different angles, one thing is particularly marked: the substitution of car parks for terraced streets, but Portland Street (1830s), bottom right in this *Echo* picture, survived the blitz to give a stucco reminder of a more stylish era.

THE PREVALENCE of big families in those days is reflected in the numbers of children who always seem to find themselves near photographer F.G.O. Stuart's ladder, here perched — how precariously we'll never know — on the cobbles of Shirley's main street. The Shirley Hotel catered at concerts, balls and banquets.

SHIRLEY HIGH STREET 1985

THERE IS much that still remains after 80-odd years. Now the pub is called the Shirley, but boasts a coat of arms and one of those curiously inappropriate signs that are springing up all over the city. Where Penton ran his corn stores there is now the local branch of Lloyds Bank.

AN EDWARDIAN reminder that where there were once large estates, and mansions to match, there are now dissecting suburban streets. These were the gates in Regents Park Road at the Shirley end. The park had another set of gates at Millbrook which lasted longer than these.

A SHORT TIME after F.G.O. Stuart took his photograph the gates were gone. But the lodge house still remains - in modernised form. Now Regents Park Road is a very busy thoroughfare. Not far from this junction are the shops of Shirley High Street and — just a Goliath sling-shot closer — a large supermarket.

TALL TOPPERS in evidence as the Rogers family pose in stylised, scattered fashion, patiently waiting for the photographer to complete his picture. Their exquisite 'cottage orne' is Red Lodge, into which the family moved about 1829. They ran Red Lodge Nurseries and also had a shop at 181 High Street.

THE COTTAGE still exists, hidden behind tall rhododendrons once admired by none other than Queen Mary. The cottage, near the Bassett Avenue–Winchester Road junction, is so secluded that one elderly Sotonian who knew it in his youth genuinely believed it had long gone. Now known as Little Oak Hall, it is the home of bookseller Bruce Gilbert, seen here with (right to left) his wife Angela, their son Richard, and Lizzie Ashworth, Richard's fiancee.

HIGHFIELD CHURCH c.1900

PINAFORED GIRLS and eton-collared boys gather aimlessly by the church wall at the dusty Church Lane junction. A later postcard, showing houses on the right, bears the message: 'I used to go to this church when I was a little girl, but there were no houses then — nothing but fields around it'.

HIGHFIELD CHURCH 1985

NOW CHRIST CHURCH, Portswood (its correct name — and where Highfield and Portswood begin and end strikes newcomers as very subtle) stands in the middle of a select suburb, facing architect Herbert Collins' garden city-style Uplands Estate — a local Hampstead where profs and lecturers munch muesli over the breakfast *Guardian*.

BELGRAVE ROAD 1919

IN THE WAR that has just ended, this local Coronation Street was reckoned to have been the most patriotic road in the town, with 108 residents from its 134 houses serving as soldiers or sailors. In those days it was honeycombed with cuts, alleys, back-ways—and 'tis said that many a lawbreaker escaped the police because of his knowledge of escape routes.

BELGRAVE ROAD 1985

HOW LIFELESS it looks today! Gone are the terraces (demolished in 1969) and in their place the yards and sheds of a trading estate. A lady who lived in the road from 1911 to 1916, Mrs. Pither, remembers a different scene full of characters . . .like the McAllan family who had a vegetable round and stabled their horse in a back bedroom in bad weather!

BEFORE THE WAR this old tarred wooden house stood in Portswood Road, east of Portswood junction, giving a touch of Scandinavia to the area. It faced the end of Brickfield Road — a name deriving from the old brickfields which, together with piggeries, once stood in the meadows at its northern end.

HOARDINGS DOMINATE the tarred house site now and some of the houses behind it have gone. Vanished, too, is the picket fence. But the wall to the left still stands — apparently having only lost one brick! — and, wondrously, one or two of the old fenceposts are still in position. Of the tarred house and its occupants, unfortunately, little is known.

IT WAS AN OLD INN when this photograph was taken by Mentor and Co., who had a studio in Oxford Street. The adjoining building, which bears the date 1903, replaced an old cottage dating from even quieter days 'afore the railway come'.

THE FLEMING ARMS 1985

STRONG'S VILLAGE PUB has now become a Beefeater steak house on the busy A27. But the hostelry, bearing the name and arms of Stoneham's squires, retains its look of coaching days—and its name, unlike several other elderly pubs recently retitled.

NOT MUCH traffic about to worry this carter with his milk churns as his horse clops by the Fleming Arms. The house at the end, like the Grange and several other old buildings hereabouts, has vanished.

PHOTOGRAPHER Patrick Brookes performed some nimble footwork to get a shot to match the one opposite. The old bridge has put in some sterling service and so has Max Headroom! Both 'tis often said, deserve retirement.

HOW OFTEN, in the old photos and cards, little girls with hoops are posed unconcernedly in the middle of the road! Today, at the junction of Portswood Lane, such posing would be impossible – or, if possible, lethal!

AT THE SAME junction today there is a steady stream of traffic, but the houses are the same. The ones on the right, though, are earmarked to go in motorway plans. The old telegraph poles have been replaced by that unlovely design of modern lamp-post described by Sir John Betjeman as looking like 'a boa constrictor being sick'.

73

BITTERNE PARK 1906

F.G.O. STUART, so beloved of postcard buffs, is said to have used ladders to get above his subjects. He was certainly high up when he took this shot in Whitworth Crescent by the Itchen. One can imagine the enterprising Scot ordering: 'Keep still, all ye children — especially you two pretending to be horses!'.

THE BUILDING on the right, the Bitterne Park Hotel, is still a popular 'watering place', and Whitworth Crescent, going into Whitworth Road, remains a pleasant suburban domain for small boat owners. It takes its name from inventor Joseph Whitworth, doubtless much admired by the directors of the Liberal Land Company who developed the 'park'.

THE DATE is imprecise, but this postcard, perhaps the most intriguing in the book, is postmarked 1909. The prospect over the river is certainly impressive — 'Southampton from Bitterne Park,' the card is titled — but the angle taken is so unusual that much exploration had to be done before the exact location was identified.

BITTERNE PARK 1985

A STROLL down Cobden Avenue revealed that the backs of the two houses on the postcard belonged to No. 29 (left), now a social services area office, and 'Linacres'. The old vicarage to the east and Church House to the west were yet to come. The older picture was presumably taken from open ground off Thorold Road but a similar view today proved impossible because of trees and buildings. The two houses, facing down Bullar Road, were identified by their rooftop ornamentation.

THE POSTCARD says 'Bitterne Village', and it really looks like a village here. The houses on the right and Bitterne School on the Bursledon Road corner have disappeared in redevelopment. All was peaceful then and people habitually walked in the middle of the road.

HIGH STREET, BITTERNE 1985

THOUGH THE main shopping area has become a precinct and the old village has literally been pulled apart to make way for a bypass, two bastions of the past remain — the church and the pub (the Red Lion on the Bursledon-Botley fork has gained a middle gable).

CHAPEL STREET, BITTERNE c.1912

IT LOOKS like a village scene from Hardy, but the magnifying glass reveals a sign for the Bitterne Cycle and Motor Works. So presumably the horseless carriage was well established. With the 1920 entry of Bitterne into the borough, some street names had to be changed and Chapel Street, in title at least, was soon to be no more.

DEAN ROAD, BITTERNE 1985

ONLY THE parish church and the white house, now next to the new leisure centre, remain from the earlier picture. Present-day Dean Road — the name change came in 1924 — looks down to the new bypass which has in places totally altered the old village. If the old man in the boater could return he wouldn't know Chapel Street!

BEYOND THE horse manure F.G.O. Stuart's customary clutch of children pose in the middle of the road, while a roundsman for Pitcher's bakers and confectioners, unmindful of the camera, is about to clamber aboard his van before setting off to 'wait on more families'.

IT'S SURPRISING how little this main Woolston thoroughfare has changed. St. Mark's Institute, next to the Fiesta food centre (right), has gained a new entrance and a butchers' shop (left) has become a bakery, the Oven Door.

'A PRETTY SCENE,' stated *The Stranger's Guide to Southampton* 50 years earlier, with its 'clear water overhung by trees and backed by a wild heath'. But this pond at the junction of two streams hasn't always been pretty and back in the 1960s letters to the local press denounced it as 'overgrown', 'evil-smelling', 'neglected' — and a receptacle for rubbish.

THINGS HAVE IMPROVED in recent years. Environmental groups and birdwatchers have taken an interest in the pond and schoolchildren have spent half-term holidays cleaning up polluted water and its surrounds. In 1984 a Miller's Pond Area Conservation Society was formed and a fight to combat building plans was begun.

WESTON LANE was once a gravelly road meandering through a quiet village on its way to the sea. The terrace on the left is no more. Neither, alas, is the charming thatched cottage on the right. In pre-motor days this was a favourite spot for strollers from all parts of the Southampton area. And there was always the Sun Hotel for a Scrase's pint.

THE SUN HOTEL, now Inn, is slightly altered, but only the ghosts of former customers quaff spectral Scrase's. In Weston Lane now there is a shopping centre and plentiful post-war housing of varying stylistic quality. Twenty years ago the one-time country lane received a £50,000 road improvement. O tempora, o mores!

IN THE LATE 1880s Mrs. Henrietta Bellenden Sayers left £1,000 — a huge sum then — for drinking fountains. A 68-entry architectural competition resulted in the Clock Tower which until 1934 stood in Above Bar before removal to Bitterne Park Triangle. There was money left over for a second fountain — the one in this photograph, now vanished, a survivor amid the blitz damage. It was put up in 1890 in 'open space at the eastern end of the Railway Carriage Bridge'.

FLOATING BRIDGE ROAD 1985

ONE OF this book's most changed scenes. The Floating Bridge, last of a long series of varied ferry services across the Itchen, carried on until the magnificent Itchen Bridge was opened on June 1st 1977. The whole area by this time had become transformed. One of the floating bridges was soon to be a Woolston disco, initially called Floaters and then the Riverside, and a locally written chart-busting single mourned the passing of 'The Woolston Ferry'.

THE LATE Charlotte Timms, who had a general stores on the corner of Forster Road and Cedar Road, poses on a sunny day in 1926 with her sons. It was the year of the General Strike, but if you wanted cheering up you could always visit the Rialto cinema in Shirley to see the Edward Everett Horton comedy *Marry Me* — an ideal film to be advertised at such a shop, for it dealt with a lover's message on an egg.

THE SHOP ON THE CORNER 1985

NOW THE SHOP is gone and in its place, behind a jungle of gorse and other plants, is Bevois Town Primary School. Of Mrs. Timms' two sons, Jack — with the glasses — died during the war, but George — now a long time in long trousers! — is alive and well and living at Dibden. Forster Road is closed to traffic at this end.

SIX DIALS c.1900

THE 'DIAL' from which the six roads fanned out is less conspicuous these days, but (going clockwise) St Mary's Road, St. Mark's Road, Northam Road, St. Mary Street, New Road and St. Andrew's Road are still with us. Many buildings came down in post-war years to make way for substantial car-parking facilities.

NOWADAYS the area is more 'cultural'. Northam Road is a centre for the antique trade and the old Bridge Tavern (on the corner of St. Mary Street—right) has become an art shop and gallery looking out not on tram lines but the inevitable car park.

EVEN ALLOWING for the licence granted to themselves by artist-engravers, this probably gives a good idea of what the area must have looked like in the middle of the last century. The engraving (by one H. Bibby), comes from Barclay's *Universal English Dictionary (Improved)*. The perspective is a little fanciful, of course.

IN THIS amalgamation of three photographs there is now no shore! The Rev. James Barclay called Southampton 'a large and handsome town pleasantly situated on a fine inlet of sea'. The city has become much larger and except for the rail tunnel, some elegant terraces and some (hidden) spires, the scene is one of almost total change.

OTHER HAMPSHIRE TITLES
AVAILABLE FROM COUNTRYSIDE BOOKS

A Hampshire Album	*Anthony Brode*	£4.95
The Hampshire Village Book	*Anthony Brode*	£4.95
Haunted Hampshire	*Anthony Brode*	£2.50
The Southampton Blitz	*Anthony Brode*	£2.95
North Hampshire Walks	*Nick Channer*	£1.95
The Unknown Forest	*Anne Marie Edwards*	£2.50
The Wayfarer's Walk	*Hampshire County Council*	£2.50
The Solent Way	*Barry Shurlock*	£2.95
Walking in Hampshire	*Hampshire County Council*	£2.50
Smuggling in Hampshire and Dorset	*Geoffrey Morley*	£4.95
Tales of Old Hampshire	*Cecilia Millson*	£3.50
A Hampshire Miscellany	*Sean Street*	£2.95
Explore Hampshire	*John Holder*	£4.95

For a complete catalogue of our publications please write to:

Countryside Books
3 Catherine Road
Newbury
Berkshire RG14 7NA